I0163546

# Thin Ice

ALSO BY ALICE KAVOUNAS FROM SHEARSMAN BOOKS

*Ornament of Asia*

THE SHEARSMAN CHAPBOOK SERIES, 2013
Martin Anderson *The Lower Reaches*
Richard Berengarten *Imagems 1*
Susan Connolly *The Sun-Artist*
Amy Evans *The Sea Quells*
Alice Kavounas *Thin Ice*
Tin Ujević *Twelve Poems (translated by Richard Berengarten)*

# Thin Ice

Alice Kavounas

Shearsman Books

First published in the United Kingdom in 2013 by
Shearsman Books
50 Westons Hill Drive
Emersons Green
Bristol
BS16 7DF


www.shearsman.com

ISBN 978-1-84861-315-7

Copyright © Alice Kavounas, 2013

The right of Alice Kavounas to be identified as the author
of this work has been asserted by her in accordance with the
Copyrights, Designs and Patents Act of 1988.
All rights reserved.

Cover: 'Missouri winter ice storm'
copyright © James Pauls, 2008.

ACKNOWLEDGEMENTS
'Seal Harbour, Maine' first appeared
in *The Times Literary Supplement*

# Contents

# Single Digit Days

January's sun punches through bare-limbed trees
like a prize-fighter's fist—splintering my windscreen.
I drive straight on, into the New Year.

What to make of the spittle-like verges
glistening along these storm-rutted lanes?
What to make of the scrappy, left-over ice
mixed with mud—the unfresh look of these
single digit days? Hard winter light

casts a tall, wobbling shadow on the brambly hedge:
horse and rider ahead. I slow
to a crawl. Young horse—CAUTION. Yes,
the horse is visibly frisky, mane-tossing fresh.
Its seasoned rider waves in my rear-view mirror.

What to make of the year ahead?
To learn, along with that young horse,
not to fear where the road leads?

# Be Me

*(After Tomas Alfredson's film 'Let the Right One In')*

*Why not be me*, she said, *just for a while.*
To satisfy his new-found friend's desire

he set up a neighbour for the next kill
who died by her knife, not his. But still. Still.

All appetite, she drank and drank.
Who are you? he ventured, though to be frank

by then he felt sure he knew.
*I*, she whispered, *am you.*

But I don't kill! *Ahhh*, she smiled,
if you could call it a smile,

if you could call her a 'she'.
*Then tell me:*

*don't you carry a knife? And plot revenge?*
That much was true. So he ran his finger

along the blade, cutting himself until he bled,
until, wild-eyed, she backed out of the room, and fled.

When that same gang of boys came after him,
when they decided to drown him,

when he could hold his breath no longer,
she reappeared, avenging him, returning the favour

at a cost he knew. And with four fresh kills
streaming in their wake, together they flew.

# The Mill Race

An eyebrow moon tonight, French. Pencil-thin.
Norman chestnut trees stand in full leaf.
Water sluicing over schist shushes me.
I turn out the lamp. My hand. The desk.
An unshuttered window. A vanishing act.
No familiar beam of the Lizard Light
blinking blinking blinking, scanning for boats
or swimmers in distress in Coverack Bay.

I pretend to be a blank sheet in a darkroom
preparing to dip myself in and out of solutions.
I'll twist and weave like a stream. Encounter rocks.
(Mistakes often produce the best results.) *Try*

*everything!* Morning. A trace of an image,
silvery as the millrace, steals onto paper.

# Seal Harbor, Maine

You must have slowed your step for me
and stooped slightly, to reach my hand.
I'm three, against your fit and weathered
fifty-three—old, in that America, for a father.

On our walks, sea met primordial rock—
crashing, ebbing, slithering through fissures
into rock pools: my mirror-bright worlds. Later, freewheeling
gulls would make off with the remains of lobster lunches.

Postcards kept arriving—close friends, cousins, colleagues,
your brother, living through the death throes of civil war.
Your already depleted country, still fighting with itself.
Here, it was croquet and iced lemonade

on the sloping lawns of the silvered clapboard mansion
whose owners had befriended you and mother. And I had
the run of it! Seal Harbor, affording you a break—
shelter from feverish heat, squalls, of that summer of '48.

# Thin Ice

The man who twirled me round each Saturday,
older than my brother, younger than my father,
was called Otto, a name like no other
within my circle of school-friends; family.

Tall, thin, thin-haired, blond, his face a long pale
oval tilted skyward, chin thrust forward,
Otto carved elegant, contiguous figure-eights
at a languid pace across this pristine,
miniature landscape of man-made ice,
in his weekly attempt to teach me

how to skate. As his pupil, I was, frankly,
something of a disappointment to us both,
not that Otto nor I ever let on
to mother. I'd attempt, but never master,
the art of skating backward, nor learn to glide
as he did, hands clasped nonchalantly

at the small of his narrow back, dreaming
perhaps, of more graceful dancing partners,
of Austria, who knows? Otto's English
remained as vestigial as my father's:

*Left foot, lift now! Now! Turn, spin. No, no, no.*
At Christmas, in the shadow of a giant spruce,
we'd celebrate with hot chocolate, topped
*mit* swirls and twirls of *Schlag*, pale Austrian-
American Otto, and Greek-American me.

On thin ice, glistening at Manhattan's heart,
we skated round and round each other,
ringed by Rockefeller's millions, Otto's
flashing blades describing dazzling figure-eights;
mine, increasingly imperfect zeroes.

# Villa Mokoras

*for Jessica*

In the demolishing heat, we read and mostly sleep away
the afternoons, on one or another of the stone terraces
where coils of fat yellow hose await the gardener's hand
to unwind and flick, unwind and flick
unleashing cool fresh water to quench the countless *pithoi*
festooned with hibiscus, oleander, geraniums—
scarlet blazing against blazing skies. Through half-lidded eyes,
I glimpse how, at intervals, he slowly raises the silver arc
of braided water, and by dipping his head toward the mouth
of the un-coiled garden snake, slakes his own unending thirst.

# The Orangerie at Penlee House, 1933

He's captured her in stark
black and white
up to her fashionable neck
in oranges—face to face with
flaming colour, inhaling that sweet tang
of the Mediterranean

here, near to where I'm sitting in the
Orangery Café nearly eighty years later,
sipping at an espresso, as black
as her slicked-back hair. She's posing artfully,
languishing amidst hot-house fruit,
or is she truly intoxicated? Each orange globe—

how it lit up the black and white winters
filling the ample toe of a Christmas stocking
which was fastened to the foot of a child's bed
or hung by the chimney breast at midnight, concealing
a precious gift to be unpeeled at dawn,
its juice the colour of the sun, rising.

Note:
Inspired by T.E. Corin's photograph 'The Orangerie at Penlee House, 1933',
and exhibited together in the 2012 Penlee Exhibition, Penzance, Cornwall.

# Hair-Trigger

You were new at work, ridiculously
handsome, though your close-cropped hair was ice-white.
It had turned, you said, practically overnight—
you and your friend were fighting side by side

when he folded at your feet, shot dead.
We'd only just met. But I stayed the night—
woke to the sight of you springing to the front
door at a sound I barely heard—was it

the elevator reaching your floor—your neighbour
coming home in the small hours? You'd reached
for something tucked under your pillow like a charm—
then leapt out of your side of the bed, returning

minutes later holding a gun. I listened
as you tried to explain how it was with you,
while I thought how it would be. Even in
your own apartment, you were on a hair-trigger.

In time, it will go back to your own colour,
the doctor had promised—jet black before
Vietnam. At dawn, I crept silently out of bed,
felt your eyes on me as I dressed quickly, and left.

# Helter Skelter

In the freezing hold, hurled helter skelter
into the dark, lie our clothes, neatly folded,
entombed in cases, the arms of jackets and sweaters
crossed loosely at the wrists, or pinned back—

fragile blouses rubbing up against fresh shirts—
buttoned up to their necks—silk ties tightly
coiled, leather shoes buffed and stuffed
under their tongues with balled up socks,

or handfuls of jewels stashed in their toes;
trouser legs all bent double—all of it travelling
in parallel, our baggage always with us,
flying blind, shadowing every journey.

We reach our destination, pluck our possessions
from the revolving belt—nearly identical cases
concealing nearly identical possessions. Later,
we unpack, unfolding and smoothing each

precisely-creased garment as if to smooth our own
stiffened arms and legs. We slip into our second skins,
check the mirror image of ourselves, and venture out
helter skelter, into the jumbled day.

# Although

Although your entry has not been awarded
one of the thirty-three top prizes, it is among the 100 long-listed
from 4,333 submitted, and you are most welcome, at your own
expense, and, regrettably, at very short notice, to celebrate…

Although your thrice-revised planning application to expand
by one meter in width and length your 1942
garage, has been turned down for the final time, may we
be so bold as to suggest a change of vehicle, such as…

Although your 19-year credit history with us remains
unblemished, your request for an additional £2,000 overdraft limit,
which at present is at the arranged rate of 7.25% over the base
rate of 0.5%, given the current economic climate, we regret is beyond our…

Although as a valued member of our company, your contract
states that your employment cannot be terminated without
either three written warnings, or without three months'
notice on either side, this is to inform you that as of tomorrow…

Although your ticket guarantees that we would, if necessary, find you an alternative airline to fly you to your destination, arriving on the same day, it transpires that the only arrangement possible is for you to take Flight B2206, arriving near the picturesque village of…

Although you hold comprehensive insurance for storm damage to your house and out-buildings, and have not claimed for 14 years, the condition of the tree which fell onto your roof, was, according to our assessors, such that it invalidates clause 64, section iii, found on page…

Although, as you correctly point out in your letter, the Care Label on our Designer Range cream 100% Linen Trouser, states: *Machine Washable Delicates 40°; Tumble Dry, Low*, we cannot be held responsible for the variable water quality in postcodes across the UK, therefore…

Although you embarked on your course of postgraduate study under the Credit Accumulation Transfer Scheme (CATS), new regulations require us to inform you that your 120 CATS, completed at Distinction level (congratulations) cannot, in fact, be transferred to any institute of higher education, neither here in the UK, nor…

# High Summer, The Lizard

The wind is shivering the broad back of our neighbour's field. I walk along
Its bumpy spine, this narrow tamped-down path that snakes through
The barley undulating on either side of me. I'm swimming
More than walking, or afloat in a small boat, my hand trailing idly,
A five-fingered comb, luxuriating in this sea of miniature plaits, each
Impossibly perfect, waving on its slender stem, *en masse*
A magical assembly of shiny schoolgirls with their neatly-plaited hair,
Appearing to greet me on this August morning. I head toward the far corner
Of the field, the stile a knuckle of old stones placed just so: one, two, three,
Jump! The wind at my back. Ahead, the path through another shimmering field.

# Neon-Green Man

Maybe he knows something. A bomb. What if
he's planted it? Under a seat. My seat.
The neon-green man's on the run, guarding
the exits. So far, no one's questioning him.

I could, if he were a common criminal, yell *Stop! Thief!*
and hope for the best. But maybe he's just an ordinary guy
who's caught the Norovirus. He's *so* green, as if he's about
to throw up. Or, as if he's been swimming in chlorine.

That could be it. An illegal Chinese immigrant—
in his head, still escaping from some factory—
poisoned from years of making jeans like these.
If that's true, I'll rip them off! Never buy them again.

On the other hand, the man doesn't look Chinese.
What if the theatre's on fire? While I nipped out
to get sweets, did I miss something? An important
announcement? What if he's that terrorist—you know—

Chemical Ali—this neon man *is* green, after all. No,
can't be him. Ali Hassan al-Mahid's been caught.
Hung. This faceless man—-could he be Kurdish?—a lucky
survivor, blinded by chemicals? He seems to appear

everywhere, yet running in place. Running and running
all over London. If he's fleeing from bush fires—in his head,
I mean—-if he's Australian, running from bush fires,
that's really sad? But smart. That's probably why he was saved.

The official Australian advice has just changed:
*Don't stay in your house. Run. Run for your life.*
*Your house isn't safe. Your house is fuel.*
Did you just feel a shudder? The imminent earthquake.

It's scheduled to occur anytime now;
definitely within the next two hundred years.
You say it's too late? Have all the men
turned green and I've only just noticed—

now when the lights are dimming, and the show's
about to begin? Should we stand up, follow
this transparent man who's green to the marrow—
or run like hell in the opposite direction?

Should we wait for further instructions
in silence, together, in the dying light?
I'm staring at the sign. What do you think?
What exactly does this glowing man know?

# Mother Goose As Moon-Rider

She's a moon-rider, sailing to the sound of goose-music,
the steady flapping of her gander's wings
beating time to the unfolding rhyme of her journey.

She's a moon-rider, sailing above the weather,
the landscape below, a child's quilt—wheat, barley and corn
stitched by streams, held firm by earth and rock
riven by storms, criss-crossed by rivers of tarmac.

Husband-less and husbander of gold, she rides on—
a white witch on her eiderdown mount
sprinkling gold dust according to her whim—or so it seems—
giving and not giving—in her conical comical hat, sailing
across a sky, blindingly blue as her dress, trailing petticoat clouds.

She's a moon-rider, fated to be hated the one day,
loved the next—holding single-handedly the single rein,
a ribbon as slender as a skein of geese, silken as her gander's
neck—a gander impossibly grand—which she guides
over the moon and back, night after night, both keeping
time to the rhyme of their journey through time.

Note: I'm indebted to Andy Brown and John Burnside for identifying Aldo
Leopold's phrase 'goose music' and for their collection *Goose Music* (Salt).

# You Might Even Learn to Fly

We have long-term sitting tenants,
though they come and go. One family occupies
our unconverted garage; the other
favours the gazebo. You'll warm to them
as they peer out from meticulously constructed
nests. The parents apologise in advance
for their fledglings. Young swallows stumbling about
will make a mess of your car and shiny mower
as they learn the necessary basics:
how to fly to Africa, and back again next Spring.

Our resident owls, whose *ho-hoo-hoo-ooooo*s
reveal a Tawny nature, choose to live
somewhere in the barns. From their undisclosed
location, they keep in check the local
rodent population. Maybe you'll be luckier,
more observant, catch sight of them unaware.
I've had to be content with picturing them
on the wing, crossing fields, weaving invisibly
through woodland, mercilessly seizing supper,
returning home at dawn to rest their owl eyes.

At noon, however grey the day, the sun
breaks through, brief and fierce, hammering the sea
into undulating bands of silver—
sheer alchemy. And on nights like this,
when the moon is full, an unearthly brightness
steals into the room, outshining every lamp,
impossible to ignore—distracting me
from the book I'm meant to be reading,
from the book I'm meant to be writing. Finally,

I should mention the pair of blackbirds, tame
and somewhat bossy. He takes his own sweet time
splish-splashing in the bath, while she looks out

for worms, idly pecking at seed scattered by finches,
sparrows, the robin. Decide to buy our place
and you'll have to put up with the neighbours,
welcome the swallows, wash your car, respect
the owls, wait your turn for the bath, attempt
to ignore the moon. You might even learn to fly.

# My Arboretum

### VALLIER

PALM *Tracycarpus fortunei*

Scissor-fingered fronds
fan out against sea and sky.
A fresh show of hands.


PLUM *Prunus domestica*

*Espaliered*, burdened
with fruit—ovoid, split, oozing.
The wasps' *déjeuner*.


CRAB APPLE *Malus x billieri*

Scarlet ornaments
hang from every wet black bough.
Christmas in July.


MYRTLE *Myrtus communis*

Depthless evergreen
set alight by summer's white.
Winter will follow.


TREE FERN *Dicksonia Antarctica*

Its Queen's wave greets each
invisible, passing breeze.
It thrills to fine rain.

FIG *Ficus carica Moraceae*

'I don't care a fig'
is hardly my view of figs.
A blackbird's delight.


OLIVE Olea europaea

Pliant branches arch
then dip, from wind-twisted trunks.
Weave me crowns of peace.

# Requiem Mass

The Benedictine Father isn't above the sharing of a small joke —a pleasantry—
as if to say, yes, I'm a man of God but tolerant of life on earth; of how and why

you, and you, might stray. He outlines the well-trodden path to salvation
open to late-comers to the faith; early defectors. The Father leaves us

in no doubt as to his belief: the body in that coffin isn't dead, as in finished,
decaying. Soul extinguished. He talks of heaven, of where that coffined-body

will go to be resurrected, to become one with mind and soul. It sounds as if
we, too, must believe heaven is a place, with much better weather than here

on this chilly afternoon. Somewhere glorious, like the South of France
in June, without the traffic; or within a gated community on an unmapped

Caribbean island: 'Here, drink this—take of my blood. Eat—take of my body,'
intones the Benedictine Father, according to scripture. Each believer partakes

of the sacrament as the choir sings *Alleluia, Alleluia, I am the living bread*
*which came down from heaven, says the Lord. If anyone eats of this bread*

*he will live forever. Alleluia.* Yet, I stay fixed in my pew. *Lord in your mercy.*
*Hear our prayer,* responds the congregation. *Commune with Christ, our saviour,*

invites the Benedictine Father, in exchange, basically, for eternal life.
It's an incredible deal! Yet I don't move. Would I, in this paradise, hear music

as heavenly as the Fauré *In Paradisium* that I'm hearing now? What of books?
Conversation? No need, I guess, for a pen, or even a crust of bread

if we're to exist incorporeally (*if anyone eats of this bread he will live forever*)
until, of course, the day of judgment, when those redeemed are resurrected.

Love, eternal love — this is the currency. But, my love, will I find you up there?
Could we, in the meantime, live on air? We're being told now to look up —

'Let your thought be on things above,' wrote St Paul to the Colossians,
'not on the things that are on the earth'. Later, as they lower you, inch

by inch into the receiving earth, freshly dug, I try, try to look up. Air.
Eons of air. I will play music, pick up my pen, try to look up; to prepare.

# Wall Street:
## Pat Bologna Gives Joe Kennedy a Shoeshine

'Thanks for the shine'—Joe shoots Pat a smile,
flips him a dime. 'My pleasure, Mr K.
See you tomorrow! Same old place, same old time.'

Numbers bandied back and forth, futures bought,
commodities sold. Long, short—day after day
the brokers' talk sounds like gibberish—
total gibberish to these shoeshine boys,
as year on year, rag and polish back and forthing,
they overhear numbers soaring, soaring.

Slowly, the jargon begins to make sense,
at least to Pat. He decides to risk
his modest stash—*Why save my cash
if this is the way to a better life?
The market's red hot. In no time I'll double,
triple my stake. Why? How? Who in hell knows?*

*Just buy. Buy.* One August morning in '29,
as Pat cradles the brogues of his regular Joe,
he proudly announces: 'Hey, Mr K,
I've been listening hard, following your leads,
investing my pay—my shares are rocketing!
When a tip comes my way, you'll be first to know.'

A strange light steals into Joe Kennedy's eye.
He flips Pat some dimes—'Thanks, pal, for the
terrific shine.' 'My pleasure, Mr K, and thanks for that tip!'
Man to man, Kennedy shakes Pat's varnished hand:
'On the contrary, Pat. The pleasure's all mine.'

Joe's a good listener; what he's heard is this:
When your shoeshine boy starts offering tips

the market's too hot. Whatever the price,
it's time to unload the whole goddam lot.

Joe doesn't waste time, takes off like a shot,
heads for the bank—sells like a demon, then
walks away, cool as a felon that August day.

September sees markets reach dizzying heights.
Joe isn't tempted. He knows what he knows.
Sure enough, the twenty-fourth October
finds Joe sitting pretty on his mountain of cash.
Unlike young Pat, who along with millions,
loses every cent of his modest stash—

gone, on Black Thursday, a.k.a. The Crash.
Young enough to start over, Pat re-joins
the ranks that began swelling that October,
the shoeshine boys with their rags and polish,
crouching at the feet of Wall Street's finest:
the suits, money makers, the movers and shakers.

# Carousel of Smells

My pup is in love with the dishwasher.
She'd like to marry it, become one with its
silvery hulk. How she lavishes attention
on its slimy innards, stares longingly
at its stack of dirty secrets, her fresh pink
tongue stealing a lick while my back is turned.

She crouches down low by its wide open mouth,
nosing as far as she dares into its cavernous depths
inhaling a carousel of smells, eyeing the dizzying
display of scrapings and encrustations:
a wedding feast fit to celebrate insatiable desire.
I click shut the dishwasher door; press 'Start'.

Exhaling a sigh of unrequited passion, she dozes off
to the electric rhythm of its hotly beating heart.

# May, *Maia, Bloumaand*

May is a poem, each blossom a syllable.

June July August, a play in three acts
performed in the round, under cerulean skies.

September is prose, sensible. Crisp. A year's gathering
of ideas, written on leaves.

October's a thriller, Danish or Swedish. Dozens of episodes, get the boxed set.
A chilling experience in the lengthening evenings.

November: Remembrance. A laying of wreaths. An unsparing memoir,
to read or to write; familial branches laid bare by the wind,
lit by the nib of a low, piercing sun.

December's a musical, all singing, all dancing,
with parts for everyone, including the donkey.

January's a blog, fresh as snow at the start,
 a slog to keep up as you slush your way through
  to the thirty-first day of this endless month.

February's flash fiction, terse and trendy
 with game-changing twists every Leap Year.

March is a screenplay, featuring a head-turning heroine
 by a writer in search of a Hollywood option.

April is fantasy: a childlike plot: an uptown girl and her downtown fella;
 floods of tears, an unhappy ending.
  A runaway best-seller.

May. A poem, each syllable a blossom.

Note:
May is from the Latin Maius, probably from Maia, goddess of growth and increase. The old Dutch name for May was *Bloumaand*, 'blossoming month'. The Anglo-Saxons called this month *thrimilce*, because cows could be milked three times a day.

# Castles in the Air, Porthmeor

It begins with a line, cast into the deep.

    You sell what you catch

        and paint in your sleep.


It begins with a line, in your mind's eye.

    I'll do this and not that,

        live here, and not there.


It begins with a line, drawn in the sand.

    You're that child again

        building castles in the air.


It begins with a line, sketched onto board.

    What you know is the sea,

        you paint what you know.


It begins with a line, as wide as your brush.

    You load it with colour

        straight from the tin.

It begins with a line, infinite as a wave.

You'll make it your own

as you ride it home.

It begins with a line, left by high tide.

You eye the horizon,

life on the margins.

It begins with a line, where sea becomes sky.

You drink in that light

till the day you die.

It will end with a line, inscribed in stone.

We're each moved to make marks,

who can say why?

*If you have built castles in the air, your work need not be lost; that is where they should be. Now put the foundations under them.*
—Henry David Thoreau (1817-1862)

www.ingramcontent.com/pod-product-compliance
Lightning Source LLC
Chambersburg PA
CBHW021948040426
42448CB00008B/1290

* 9 7 8 1 8 4 8 6 1 3 1 5 7 *